Author:
Meredith Costain is a full-time writer and
editor of books and magazines for children. Her
many titles range from picture books through to
popular fiction and nonfiction for older readers.
She lives in Melbourne, Australia, with her partner,
fellow children's writer Paul Collins.

Artist:
David Antram was born in Brighton, England,
in 1958. He studied at Eastbourne College of Art
and then worked in advertising for fifteen years
before becoming a full-time artist. He has
illustrated many children's non-fiction books.

Series creator:
David Salariya was born in Dundee, Scotland.
He has illustrated a wide range of books and has
created and designed many new series for
publishers both in the UK and overseas. In 1989,
he established The Salariya Book Company. He
lives in Brighton with his wife, illustrator Shirley
Willis, and their son Jonathan.

Editor:
Michael Ford

Published in Great Britain in 2005 by
Book House, an imprint of
The Salariya Book Company Ltd
25 Marlborough Place, Brighton BN1 1UB

Please visit the Salariya Book Company at:
www.salariya.com

ISBN 1 904642 77 2

A catalogue record for this book is available
from the British Library.

Printed and bound in China.
Printed on paper from sustainable forests.

Visit our website at **www.book-house.co.uk**
for free electronic versions of:
You wouldn't want to be an Egyptian Mummy!
You wouldn't want to be a Roman Gladiator!
Avoid joining Shackleton's Polar Expedition!
Avoid sailing on a 19th-century Whaling Ship!

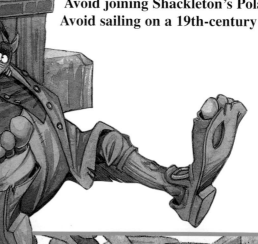

Avoid being a Convict sent to Australia!

The Danger Zone

Written by
Meredith Costain

Illustrated by
David Antram

Created and designed by
David Salariya

BOOK HOUSE

Contents

Introduction

I t's 1785 and you're the son of a farm labourer in England. Like his father and grandfather before him, your father has been growing crops on a tiny strip of rented land on a farm west of London. But now the lord of the local manor has decided he wants all the land for himself. Recent laws passed by the British Government, called the Enclosure Acts, allow him to fence off a large area of land, including your patch. There is no longer any work for your family and you are all starving. You hear there is plenty of work available in the new factories opening up in London, so you move there in search of a better life. You have no idea that in a few months' time, this move will eventually take you to the other end of the earth.

From country to city

CITY LIFE. Many people are forced to live in tiny, filthy houses, without toilet facilities. Instead, people throw their sewage straight out onto the streets.

 nce you arrive in the city you realise you have made a huge mistake. The streets are swarming with unemployed people who, like you, have flocked to the city from the country looking for work. Besides farmers, there are craftspeople who once made cloth and goods such as shoes in their cottages. Now their jobs have been taken over by spinning and weaving machines set up in large factories in the towns.

TEXTILE factories are set up in the 1770s to make cloth from wool, cotton and silk. Children as young as six work 16-hour days in appalling conditions.

RAT CATCHERS prowl the city's filthy streets and alleys. At least this is one occupation where there is always plenty of work!

People face a daily battle with hunger, dirt and disease, caused by crowded slums and streets filled with rats, rubbish and open sewers. Many die of typhus and cholera and are only buried in shallow graves. The smell is overpowering!

Poverty... disease... unemployment... how will I survive in this place?

Handy hint

Stay away from the cities – try and find work on a large country estate instead.

7

Crime...

All around you are men and women who have turned to crime to feed and clothe themselves and their families. The streets are filled with pickpockets and thieves, known as 'tail-buzzers', 'dead lurkers' and 'noisy-racket men'. In the country, the poor steal from the grand estates of the rich, and highwaymen hold up coaches on main roads.

There is no official police force to restore law and order, only occasional night patrols by nightwatchmen and parish officers, known as 'beadles'. You hear that the magistrate and novelist Henry Fielding has set up a small group of thief-catchers known as the 'Bow Street Runners'. To help deal with the crime wave, over 150 crimes are made hanging offences.

A TALL ORDER. There are only eight Bow Street Runners (above), and over a hundred thousand criminals to catch!

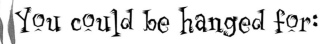

You could be hanged for:

ARSON – Deliberately setting fire to a house or a barn containing corn.

IMPERSONATING an Egyptian.

CUTTING DOWN an ornamental shrub from a garden.

SHOWING a sooty face on the highroad.

...And punishment

**D**riven to desperation by cold and hunger, you begin picking the pockets of rich folk on their way to the theatre, stealing silver snuff boxes and gold watches. A 'fence' in the next slum gives you enough money to buy food and lodging for a couple of days. The first few times it's easy. But one day you slip up and are caught by a beadle. You're rushed away to a holding cell, to await your trial at the Old Bailey. On the way you pass a gang of street urchins throwing rotten fruit at a convict in the stocks. He's the lucky one. Around the corner, a huge crowd has turned up to jeer at five poor wretches dangling from ropes at a public execution.

Make sure you don't hang around at the scene of the crime.

PRISONERS ARE FLOGGED in the streets so that others can see what becomes of thieves and pickpockets.

Splat

PRISONS (left) are dark, damp, solitary places. Prisoners are shackled to the wall with chains.

PICKPOCKETS sometimes have their hands burned with a hot branding iron (right) to convince them not to try it again.

CONDEMNED prisoners are often paraded through the streets in open carts before being strung up on the gallows to be hanged (above).

11

The Old Bailey

You sit in a courtroom surrounded by important looking lawyers and well-fed judges with long flowing hair and robes. This is London's central Criminal Court, known as the 'Old Bailey'. The judges listen carefully to the charges against you, before deciding your sentence.

You gasp – you have been sentenced to death by hanging, just for stealing a few items from rich men's pockets! But you are lucky. King George III's ministers have the power to review all death penalties. Your family petitions the King to be merciful and some time later, after an anxious wait in prison, you are told your death sentence has been changed – to seven years' transportation to the colonies.

ZZZZZZ...

Crimes and Sentences:

GEORGE BARRINGTON (aged 35), pickpocket. Transported for seven years for stealing a gold watch.

HENRY ABRAMS (aged 26), labourer. Transported for highway robbery of clothing and 15 shillings.

ESTHER ABRAHAMS (aged 15), milliner. Transported for seven years for trying to steal a bolt of silk lace.

JOHN HUDSON (aged 9), chimney sweep. Transported for seven years for burglary.

ELIZABETH MASON (aged 20). Transported for fourteen years for stealing 15 guineas.

JOHN HENRY PALMER. Transported for life for committing forgery. Died at sea.

13

Hulk Hell

There's one small problem – there's nowhere to transport you to! For many years, convicts have been sent away from Britain because there aren't enough gaols to hold them all. Most were sent to work as slave labour on plantations in the American colonies. But after the American War of Independence a new destination has to be found. Until that happens, you and your fellow convicts will be kept on a floating prison called a hulk. These are rotting old navy ships, moored on the River Thames near London. The warden tells you it's only a 'temporary solution'. But don't get too excited – some of your fellow inmates have already been here for years.

HARD LABOUR. During the day, convicts come ashore and perform hard labour in work gangs. They are expected to earn the money it costs to keep them on the hulks.

AT NIGHT convicts are chained up in overcrowded, rat-ridden, filthy cells. One in five dies from diseases such as typhus.

The First Fleet

After two years on a hulk, the government decides to 'dump' convicts in Botany Bay – a new colony on the other side of the world. On 13th May, 1787, you and 771 other convicts set sail from England. At first you live in tiny cages below decks, wearing leg irons to prevent escape. Later you're let up on deck for fresh air and exercise. The rocking of the boat makes you seasick. The food is mouldy and full of maggots and weevils. Some of your mates don't survive and are buried at sea.

NORTH ATLANTIC OCEAN

EUROPE

Portsmouth 13th May, 1787

Tenerife 3rd-10th June, 1787

AFRICA

SOUTH AMERICA

SOUTH ATLANTIC OCEAN

Rio de Janeiro 5th August – 4th September, 1787

Cape Town 13th October – 12th November, 1787

The ships of the fleet:

The Sirius (*the flagship of the fleet – a warship carrying 14 guns*)

Scarborough – *418 tonnes, male convicts*

TRANSPORT SHIPS

Charlotte – *345 tonnes, male and female convicts*

Prince of Wales – *333 tonnes, male and female convicts*

Alexander – *452 tonnes, male convicts only*

Lady Penrhyn – *338 tonnes, female convicts only*

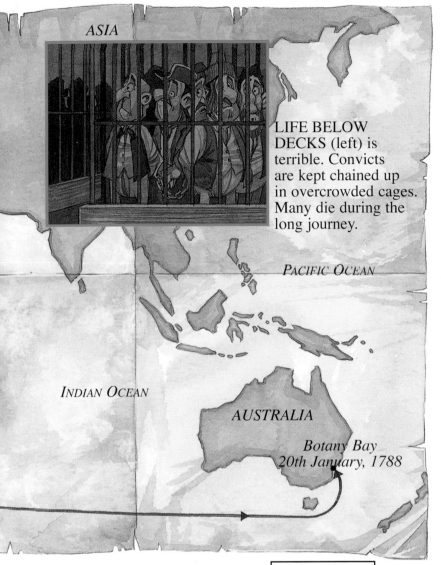

ASIA

LIFE BELOW DECKS (left) is terrible. Convicts are kept chained up in overcrowded cages. Many die during the long journey.

PACIFIC OCEAN

INDIAN OCEAN

AUSTRALIA

Botany Bay
20th January, 1788

Handy hint

Check your food carefully for weevils and maggots.

Food and clothing:

FOOD ON BOARD a convict ship includes beef and pork, dried peas, oatmeal, flour, cheese, vinegar and ship's biscuits. Male convicts are allowed the following clothes: two jackets, one pair of breeches, one waistcoat, two shirts, two pairs of shoes and stockings and one hat (below).

Friendship –
278 tonnes,
male and female
convicts

STORE SHIPS

Golden Grove –
331 tonnes

Supply – a sloop
carrying 8 guns
and additional
supplies

Fishburn –
378 tonnes

Borrowdale –
272 tonnes

17

A new home

After eight weary months of travelling, you finally arrive at your destination – Botany Bay. You can't wait to get off the ship and feel solid ground under your feet. However, Governor Phillip, the officer in charge of the fleet, decides the place you've landed isn't suitable for a settlement.

You sit on your boat for another week while a search party scours the coast for a deeper harbour.

On 26th January, 1788, you reach your new home – Sydney Cove. You start work immediately, unloading stores, clearing trees and shrubs, and pitching tents. You struggle to stand up – after three years living on boats your leg muscles have weakened. The poor food on the sea voyage has given you scurvy.

Keep moving –
we'll soon sort out
those sea-legs!

NEW NEIGHBOURS. The local people are friendly at first, but soon there are stabbings and deaths on both sides.

Handy hint

Make friends with the local Aboriginal people, who will help you to find food in the new settlement.

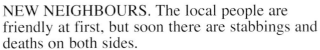

THE FIRST FLAG. Governor Phillip hoists the Union Jack to show other nations that the British are the new 'owners' of the land.

Work

Y ou are split into two groups – 'assigned convicts' clear land and work on farms; 'government convicts' carve roads and open spaces for the new colony. You tell the officers that you have farming experience and are made an assigned convict. Others are not so lucky and are made to work in a road chain gang. They break solid rock with a pickaxe all day under the hot sun. Anyone who faints from exhaustion is flogged until they get back to work.

Assigned Convicts:

WOMEN COOK, clean and work as lady's maids, while men clear and fence land, plant and harvest crops and tend sheep.

Government Convicts:

MEN CUT TIMBER, break ground to plant crops and build houses and roads. Women weave cloth and work in orphanages or hospitals.

Handy hint

Work just enough to keep on the right side of the overseer and avoid a flogging or a stint on the chain gang.

24

Floggings and chain gangs

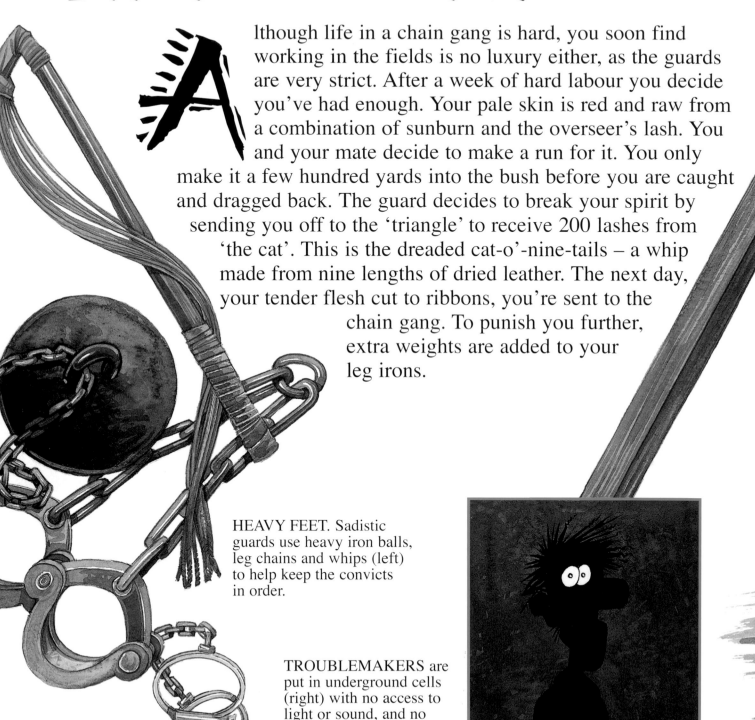

Although life in a chain gang is hard, you soon find working in the fields is no luxury either, as the guards are very strict. After a week of hard labour you decide you've had enough. Your pale skin is red and raw from a combination of sunburn and the overseer's lash. You and your mate decide to make a run for it. You only make it a few hundred yards into the bush before you are caught and dragged back. The guard decides to break your spirit by sending you off to the 'triangle' to receive 200 lashes from 'the cat'. This is the dreaded cat-o'-nine-tails – a whip made from nine lengths of dried leather. The next day, your tender flesh cut to ribbons, you're sent to the chain gang. To punish you further, extra weights are added to your leg irons.

HEAVY FEET. Sadistic guards use heavy iron balls, leg chains and whips (left) to help keep the convicts in order.

TROUBLEMAKERS are put in underground cells (right) with no access to light or sound, and no contact with other people.

Say hello to the cat!

Handy hint

Don't cry out during a flogging, because it is the code of the convicts to give the authorities the silent treatment.

REPEAT OFFENDERS. Convicts who reoffend are forced to perform hard labour on road gangs, chained at the ankles so that they can't escape.

23

Secondary penal settlements

Your life is easy compared to the hardship endured by convicts sent to secondary penal settlements. These are set up in the 1800s in new colonies in other parts of the country. The men sent there have repeatedly broken the rules of the new colony. Nothing seems to stop them – not even 'the cat'. The governors decide the only way to keep order is to use a deterrent so severe, the convicts would obey the rules rather than risk going to a new settlement. New colonies are run by cruel, sadistic men who treat the convicts like animals. Some are so desperate to escape their misery, they form suicide pacts.

WESTERN AUSTRALIA

Toodyay (Perth)

IN PORT ARTHUR, Captain Charles O'Hara Booth (right) believes that flogging makes heroes of convicts among their mates. Instead, he isolates troublemakers in underground 'dog kennels'. Convicts are also forced to walk long distances carrying bags of heavy rocks (left).

MORETON BAY. Patrick Logan (right) overworks and underfeeds the convicts in his charge. Many become sick and die. Men are tied to stones (opposite) or to the walls of their cells. Logan's cruelty earns him the nickname 'the Beast of Moreton Bay'.

Handy hint

Keep your head down and stay out of trouble!

NEWCASTLE AND NORFOLK ISLAND. Major James Morriset's (right) favourite form of punishment is the treadmill. Prisoners are chained to it for days at a time. If they stop moving, they will be crushed to death.

Moreton Bay (Brisbane)

NEW SOUTH WALES

Port Macquarie

Coal River (Newcastle)

Sydney

Norfolk Island

VAN DIEMEN'S LAND

Macquarie Harbour

Maria Island

Hobart

Port Arthur

Escape!

Every week you hear of convicts who have tried to escape. Most meet unhappy endings. Even those who manage to elude the guards find out quickly that they have no idea how to survive in the bush.

Some return to the settlement – driven back by hunger, and fear of wild animals or natives they have seen. One exception is William Buckley. He escapes from the Sorrento settlement in 1803 and spends the next 33 years living with local Aborigines. Port Arthur is the hardest settlement from which to escape. It is separated from the mainland by a narrow strip of land, which is heavily guarded by soldiers and fierce dogs, waiting to sink their fangs into juicy prisoners.

William and Mary Bryant:

CONVICTS William and Mary Bryant, their two children and seven friends escape in a stolen boat in 1791. They get as far as Dutch Timor (near Indonesia) before being caught.

GETAWAY! Most convicts who try to escape are either recaptured by guards or drown before they reach the mainland.

Billy Hunt's Folly:

FAIR GAME? Billy Hunt disguises himself in a kangaroo-skin 'suit' to sneak past the infamous line of dogs at Port Arthur. Unluckily for him, the guards decide to use the 'kangaroo' as target practice and shoot him down.

Handy hint

If you manage to escape, learn to live like the Aborigines – it will help you to survive.

Growl

Snarl

Hobart Town

Port Arthur

line of fierce dogs

Free at last

You've worked hard for three years. For this the governor grants you a conditional pardon. You are given a small plot of land and settle back into farming.

The back-breaking work of the road gang is finally over. You long to return to England to see your family, but this is not allowed. Only those granted absolute pardons may leave the colony.

You meet a young woman, Lizzie, who has earned a ticket-of-leave for good behaviour. She works for wages, but has less freedom to move about the colony. When her own pardon comes through, you will both be free to start a new life together.

A Ticket-of-leave

A Certificate of Freedom

FRANCIS GREENWAY. Transported for 14 years for forgery, Francis Greenway (below) is Australia's first qualified architect. As a convict, he designs buildings and churches for the new colony. The governor is so pleased, he grants him a pardon after only five years.

Handy hint

Keep out of trouble, and you'll receive a conditional pardon or a ticket-of-leave before your sentence is up.

MOLLIE MORGAN. Dressmaker Mollie Morgan (left) is transported for stealing cloth. After being granted a ticket-of-leave she runs a farm and a wine shop. She soon becomes a wealthy businesswoman and philanthropist.

MARY REIBEY. Mary Reibey (right) is transported for stealing a horse when she is 13. She becomes Australia's first successful businesswoman, running both a shipping firm and a warehouse (as well as having seven children!).

29

Glossary

Beadle An officer of a local parish who helped to round up thieves and pickpockets.

Cat-o'-nine-tails A knotted whip made from nine strips of dried leather. Its marks resembled the scratch marks of a cat.

Cholera An infectious, often fatal disease, with symptoms such as cramps, vomiting and diarrhoea.

Convict A person who has been found guilty of a crime and sentenced for it.

Colony A settlement or region politically controlled by a distant or 'parent' country.

Dead lurkers Nickname for people who would steal coats and umbrellas from hallways in the dim light of early evening.

Deterrent Something bad enough to stop people from acting in a certain way, for fear of the consequences.

Enclosure Acts Laws passed by Britain that allowed land-owners to fence open land, which peasant farmers had cultivated.

Fence A person who receives and sells stolen property.

Gallows A structure made from two upright posts and a crosspiece, from which a person is hanged until dead.

Highwaymen Thieves who roamed the main roads and held up coaches to steal money and personal possessions from their passengers.

Hulks Old, rotting, former naval ships which were moored in rivers and estuaries around London to house convicts.

Impersonating Pretending to be someone else.

Noisy-racket men Nickname for thieves who stole china and glass from outside of china shops.

Petition To make a formal request to a legal authority.

Philanthropist A person who does good deeds for the benefit of others.

Sadistic Gaining enjoyment from causing others pain.

Scurvy A disease caused by a lack of Vitamin C in the diet.

Slums Run-down, cramped, filthy housing in the poorest part of the city.

Stocks A wooden frame fitted with holes for the prisoner's feet. Offenders would be locked in the stocks as punishment for committing a crime.

Tail-buzzers Nickname for thieves who stole purses and snuff-boxes from people's coat pockets.

Ticket-of-leave A document that allowed convicts to work for an employer and receive wages.

Transportation Sending criminals overseas as a form of punishment.

Treadmill A huge wheel fitted with horizontal boards, used to turn the grindstones that crushed grain into flour. Convicts were chained to them and forced to work for up to 14 hours at a time.

Typhus An infectious disease transmitted by lice and fleas. Typhus patients are very weak and break out in red spots.

Index